HURTING FROM THE INSIDE

A VIEW FROM THE PEW

KAREN V. GREENE

Hurting from the Inside
Copyright © 2022 by Karen V. Greene

All rights reserved. No part of this publication may be reproduced, distributed, or transmitted in any form or by any means, including photocopying, recording, or other electronic or mechanical methods, without the prior written permission of the author, except in the case of brief quotations embodied in critical reviews and certain other non-commercial uses permitted by copyright law.

ISBN
978-1-957378-12-1 (Hardcover)
978-1-957378-11-4 (Paperback)
978-1-957378-10-7 (eBook)

Dear Pastor,

I love church, but over the years as I grew in Christ, I began to like church less. Church life left me confused. What I learned in church conflicted with what I was taught in church. So when I began to apply the things I was taught to the broken places in my life, I failed to see the point, and I was left asking, "What should I do when s.h.i.t.t. happens in my life?"

First, allow me to explain the intentional use of such a derogatory acronym. I pondered for months to find an appropriate word that aptly describes the situations I have encountered. Unfortunately, the only word that resonated in my mind is one that is not found in the Bible. Each time I tried to camouflage the harshness of reality, I felt guilty of once again compromising my true feelings to make others comfortable. Therefore, I felt compelled to replace it without losing the commonality that I want to convey.

I know the correct Christian term is *storm*, but I need you to understand that the connotation is far more important than the denotation in this message. I know that profanity just shows one's lack of intelligence in his ability to communicate what one has to say. So please, allow me to explain why an intelligent person would choose the acronym s.h.i.t.t. over storm.

S.H.I.T.T.

In Ephesians 4:29, Paul writes to the church in Ephesus, "Don't use foul or abusive language. Let everything you say be good and helpful, so that your words will be an encouragement to those who hear them" (Life Application Study Bible NLT).

As a Christian and an educator, I have made this a daily practice. Though I am not perfect, I purposely avoid using profanity–most of the time. When I am having a conversation with close friends or family, I may intentionally use a word for special effects. Being in a constant position of a role model, I understand one's concern for my decision to stand firm on using an unpleasant acronym. My true intention is to inform—not to offend. I am choosing to be open and candid so that one will truly understand the confusion that so many of us quietly experience. Therefore, I will not mask the ugliness the acronym represents.

S.H.I.T.T. simply stands for "several hurtful incidents taking a toll." These are the things in life that we are often told to "just get over it." We all have to endure some pain, but if not dealt with correctly, it accumulates. Some things in life we have no control over. Some things we have to learn to accept. (Like the old saying goes, "Change the things you can, accept the things you cannot. Have the wisdom to know the difference.") No one would argue that life is fair because it isn't. In life, s.h.i.t.t. happens. S.H.I.T.T. usually isn't fair. It's sometimes just our lot in life. I have learned how to deal with the storms in my life. It's the s.h.i.t.t. that I find difficult to handle.

Storms

A storm is defined as a "violent disturbance of the atmosphere with strong winds and usually rain, thunder, lightning, or snow".

Religious people often refer to periods of trials and tribulations (whether sickness, loss of a job, marital troubles, disobedient or troubled children, drug addiction, etc.) as storms in their lives.

During a literal storm, one may seek shelter to protect himself from this violent disturbance. For religious people, this shelter is God. God has the power to hide and protect us that we may continue to have peace in the midst of our trials (i.e., storm).

No one illustrates this better than Paul in the book of Acts 27. On his way to Rome, Paul and the other prisoners and their capturers are caught in a violent storm at sea. Although Paul warns them of the impending dangers, the centurion dismisses his warnings and decides to set sail anyway. Once the storm rages and the crew lose all control of the ship, they become frightened and hopeless. Here, Paul is not worried because an angel of God spoke to him and assured him that no life would be lost during this journey. Paul knows that if God has plans for him on the other side of the storm, He must safely bring him through the storm. Although this storm could have been avoided if they had only listened to a messenger of God, He was still faithful to bring them out unharmed. Paul is able to stand worry free because he knows God's will for his life is greater than any storm. Paul's demonstration of God's peace during the storm causes those around him to also seek God's presence in their lives. Although Paul is merely a prisoner and considered the least among them, this act of faith leads his capturers to Christ.

During the time of a storm, we can also recall the miracle that Jesus performed in Mark 4:35–41. In this passage, a storm on the ocean threatens the lives or at least the safety of those aboard the ship. Jesus simply speaks to the storm and the storm ceases, no hocus pocus and no exaggerated speech.

As a Christian, I have been taught to follow Jesus's example. Instead of talking about my storm or describing the storm as the disciples do in this passage, I should speak to the storm and tell my storm to cease. Move, there is power in the tongue. We can speak defeat, or we can speak victory over our storms and circumstances. There will be times when we have to wait, but waiting requires trust and builds faith. The important part is how we wait.

The disciples chose to complain and doubt. They quickly forgot the miracles Jesus has already done before them. They misplaced their focus as so many of us do during our storms. We must remember to focus on God and believe he has a positive and expectant end for us. We must keep our thoughts on the one who has the power to heal, save, and deliver. God can handle all of our storms.

As with many Southern African-Americans, I grew up in the church. As an adult, I worked earnestly and willingly in the church. I took joy in being a peacemaker, giver, servant, volunteer, and a teacher. Yes, pastor, I was trying to be the perfect member. See from childhood we are taught to be good and to do good. We are taught to do good and good things will come back to you. The "you reap what you sow" factor. Most Bible-based churches do an efficient job of teaching followers of Christ what to do when storms arise in their lives. We are taught to:

- Trust in the Lord with all your heart… (see Proverbs 3:5–6)
- Pray without ceasing (see 1 Thessalonians 5:17)
- God keeps his promise. Know that God's plans are good. He plans to give you a future and a hope… (see Jeremiah 29:10–13)
- Cast your cares upon Jesus (see 1 Peter 5: 6–8)

- Have faith with expectancy (see Hebrews 11)
- Praise God during the storm (see Psalm 66:8–12; Luke 5:1–11)
- Wait on the Lord and be of good courage… (see Psalm 27:13–14)
- Speak life on your situation (see Proverbs 18:21)
- Call on the elders of the church (see James 5:13–15)
- Know that God calls his children to be different. We are not to blend in with the ways of the world (see 1 Peter 2:9).
- Although not directly biblical, "When things are down, look up!"

The list of encouraging passages is endless.

I believe in praising God during the storm. I know it is just a test. I know tests draw us closer to God. Hebrews12:6–7 states, "God disciplines those he loves, and even scourges, every son whom He accepts and welcomes to His heart and cherishes. You must submit to and endure correction for discipline; God is dealing with you as with sons. For what son is there whom his father does not train and correct and discipline?" (Amplified Bible). Simply put, God tests those he loves. So I'm learning to count it all joy when I encounter one of life's test. I know tests come to strengthen my relationship with God.

My favorite scripture is Galatians 6:9, "And let us not be weary in well doing: for in due season we shall reap, if we faint not." I have used this scripture so many days when I wanted to give up or just stop. It has kept me going even when I felt I had nothing left to give. God's promise to bless those who stay in the race gives me hope. This has been another storm changer for me.

The Bible also provides countless examples of people such as Abraham, Joseph, Queen Esther, David, the woman with an issue of blood, Daniel in the lion's den, the three Hebrew boys, the Samaritan woman at the well, Peter, James and John fishing all night, and many others who were faced with challenges and how they overcame them through trust, faith, and the help of the Lord. We also see through the lives of countless Bible figures that even when our storm is a result of our own disobedience, God is still there to love us as though we have never sinned.

> Thomas saith unto him, Lord, we know now whither thou goest; and how can we know the way? Jesus saith unto

him, I am the way, the truth, and the life: no man cometh unto the Father, but by me. If ye had known me, ye should have known my Father also: and from whom henceforth ye know him, and have seen him. (John 14:5–7)

As mentioned before, life isn't fair by any definition. We each have our own cross to bear, our path to walk, our trials to overcome. My path may not look like your path. My trials may not look like your trials. My sin may not look like your sin. Yet, we all strive to make it to the same heaven.

What do those of us do when unfair is our lot? When we have to fight for things that others take for granted? Or we have to learn life's lessons through experience because of lack of earthly guidance?

In school, I see children who realize by the age of five that life isn't fair, so they act out in anger, seeking the attention and love they know they deserve, or they see other children receiving, leading them to ask the question, "What's wrong with me?" Unfortunately, these children are met with the usual response—more correction and disappointment. They are met with more isolation and the feeling that they are unworthy or they don't belong in the school environment. After all, the school environment works best for those who come from the traditional two-parent household—a factor that the typical five-year-old does not control.

Thankfully, with the right guidance, mentoring, and clear expectations and moreover, self-determination, many of these children are able to successfully adjust and flourish in school. Many learn and adopt the image of success or "right living" that school and society project. (Don't misunderstand, success and living right are real. But too many of us falsely project the image of success and right living to hide the fact that our lives are a mess and we do not have it all together, but as long as nobody knows, it's all good. For many of these children, school is an escape, a way out as it should be. School should be a source of hope for children.) Those that do not adopt this ideology are given alternative paths for their education, or they simply give up and drop out on their own.

This pattern is replicated in today's church. Many come to church seeking a better life only to be met with judgment and misunderstanding. If a purpose of the church is to bring in the lost, why are we so quick to condemn the lost and shut them out because they do not represent the ideal church or the ideal Christian? Like children who feel they do not fit in or it is too much work, many people soon give up and quit. Like children who feel they do not need school, or school isn't for them, people feel they do not need church, or it isn't for them.

I, too, do not represent the church's idea of a godly family. My children have three different fathers. My oldest is the result of a teenage pregnancy. My second child is from my ex-husband. (See, marriage does not erase the sin. It only masks it for a short time—for me, a year and a half.) My third child is the result of my Sarah complex. (I'm getting old, God. I want a child right now! Never mind, I got this.)

After countless years of church, no matter how hard I try, I do not feel as if I belong here. I do not fit the image of most Christians' tidy world. My life is sometimes a mess. I have spent years trying to serve as God would have me to serve, only to see that these very acts conflict with the world's and many Christians' view of success. I do not have the traditional family life. Like most Americans, my plan was to graduate from college, start my career, buy a house, marry Mr. Right, and have 3.5 kids, and a dog named Buster.

I do have the college degrees. I do have a house. I do have a great teaching career, three wonderful children, and a dog (the name Buster lost to Cupcake). See God still blessed me in the midst of my mess. I will never deny that.

I have been in church all my life. Church is hard. Correction, church-folks are hard. We are unforgiving. We are judgmental. I am not saying these things on the outside looking in. I am saying these things from the inside looking out.

I have watched ex-drug dealers try to rejoin the church. They soon leave. We didn't truly forgive them. I have watched ex-drug addicts try to rejoin the church. They soon leave. We didn't truly accept them. I have watched ex-cons return to church to be encouraged and start a new life in Christ. They soon leave. We didn't truly welcome them. Unfortunately, this is why many people choose to wait until they think they have somewhat fixed the stumbling block or the sin in their lives before coming to church. They want to be accepted. They want to belong. They want to be worthy of the love in which they seek.

Of course, this is almost impossible in church because all of the sins previously mentioned deem us unfit to represent the body of Christ. Therefore, we find ourselves working in vain because we erroneously seek the approval of man instead of God. As a result, like the child who eventually realizes he/she will never measure up in school, we, too, simply give up and drop out of church.

So here I am in this place where I know I am blessed and love Christ. I have a lot to offer the body of Christ. I freely give my talents to the upbuilding of God's kingdom. Yet I am still limited within the walls of the church. I will never truly be accepted by the church. Like David, "I know my transgressions, and my sin is ever before me" (Psalm 51:3). I am a sinner saved by His grace by a God who truly gives second chances to anyone. Because He has given me a second chance, I refuse to continue to live a lie. I refuse to hide my imperfections. I refuse to let my life's lessons be in vain.

Although you may accept my works, my contributions, and my talents, you do not truly accept me. You cannot see past my circumstances. You cannot see past my past. You cannot see me.

I am writing these thoughts to break free from the emotional prison I have elected to reside in for so many years. I want to be free. I need to be free from all of the innocent comments and judgments that life has made, and I adopted them as true. I need to be free from all of my s.h.i.t.t.

The Lessons My S.H.I.T.T. Has Taught Me

Lesson 1: "Second Class Citizens"— Don't Let People Count You Out!

"And Nathanael said unto him, 'Can there any good thing come out of Nazareth?' Philip saith unto him, 'Come and see'" (John 1:46).

Growing up, I had a blessed childhood. Although I knew my family was a little different from the typical family at this time, I still felt fortunate. I had great friends. I had a great extended family who supported one another. I was always able to participate in any school activity or function that interested or pertained to me. My family supported our educational efforts.

The summer before my fifth-grade year, my mother took the opportunity to finally move out on her own. She moved my siblings and me to a neighboring community fifteen miles away. Being the oldest of five siblings, I had new responsibilities. I took pride in helping watch my siblings when my mom was at work. Today we still laugh at the infamous five braids I would routinely do on my sisters' hair and the cereal with "just the right amount" of milk. I knew my mother worked hard, so I wasn't about to waste any milk. That jug had to last for the week!

During that time, the term latchkey kids became popular. Stay-at-home moms were becoming a thing of the past, and more and more kids were returning home after school to an empty house. That was quite different from what I was accustomed to at my grandparents' home. Still, I was able to find the silver lining. I had a newfound independence. I didn't mind being a latchkey kid. Actually, I loved it. I felt independent and responsible. I took my duties as the oldest and "the protector of the house until Mom gets home" seriously. I wore the pants, well, at least the shorts.

We lived there for three years until my mom could no longer afford the house. (I later learned that it was the result of an adjustable mortgage rate. In three years, my mom's mortgage payment had almost doubled. Note to self: do not agree to an adjustable mortgage rate—fixed only.)

The summer before my eighth-grade year, we moved back home. My mom was able to rent a trailer about two miles from my grandparents' home. The closeness was nice. Still, it was hard to once again leave familiar faces and make a new start. At least that time, the faces would be somewhat familiar.

Unfortunately, the biggest change was yet to come. During our move, my mom had an admirer. I would notice him drive particularly slow as he passed our house. He had stopped a few times to speak to my mom while he remained in the car. She would later announce to us that he would be our new dad. At fourteen, I knew that it was going to be an epic fail. At fourteen, I had already adopted the world's view. What did the young man want with my much older mom with five children? The answer is somewhere to lay his head. Although I was happy for my mom because I knew she wanted a husband, I immediately hated the thought of someone disturbing my lifestyle. I loved my family just the way it was flaws and all. I didn't have a daddy, and I didn't want one then, especially one that raised eyebrows. Our life was hard enough as it was. I saw him as an addition to the problem—not the solution. Life with a stepfather provided me with more entries to add to my *things-not-to-do* list. So I would just go with the old saying, if you can't say anything nice, don't say anything at all! On that note, I will simply fast-forward through the next two years of my life.

Transitions

The summer my grandfather died, I was staying with my grandparents. I could not recall why, but I was there. My grandfather was the main father figure in my life. He was the male I affectionately called Daddy. The only other father figure that ever took an active part in my life was estranged from me at that time. He was a man my mother met after moving back home. After I was told that he wasn't really my father, I didn't understand what type of relationship to have with him. (Now looking back, what young child would? I don't think he quite knew either.)

At the end of the same summer, it was time to go home. I didn't want to go. My mother was then married, and I felt that my new stepfather had taken my *supporting* role. My mother no longer needed me. I could now step out of the role of big sister/babysitter— second-in-charge—and into the role of a teenager.

My grandmother shared the news with my mom that I wanted to permanently stay with my grandmother. My mother disagreed with my decision. I watched as they exchanged opinions. When asked why I did not want to go back home, I simply replied that I just wanted to stay with my grandmother. I wasn't strong enough to say the truth—I no longer felt that I belonged there.

Moment of Truth: Although I put on a brave front, it always hurt when I saw my siblings interact with their dads—no matter how sporadic the relationships were. I envied their relationships. (I don't know if the brave front was for them or for me.) I would have traded places with them in a minute to have a dad that only brought two cans of milk for twins to consume in a month's time rather than a dad who didn't feel the need to call to see if I were a boy or a girl. I would have loved to have had a dysfunctional relationship with my dad. To a child, that was better than no relationship at all. I figured that if I removed myself from the situation, the pain would go away. I wouldn't see what I was missing.

As I listened to my mom, who was visibly upset, explain why I should return home, I can recall waiting patiently to hear her say, "Because she's my daughter, and she should be with me" or simply "because I want her." I kept waiting. Instead, I heard, "Who's going to help me watch the kids" and "She's my help." Although I knew without a doubt that my mom really loved me, at that moment, I needed to hear it. I wanted to be more than the big sister/babysitter or the help. I wanted to be her child whom she wanted to stay with her because I was hers. I never got to hear it that night. I felt bad about leaving my siblings, but I was ready to embrace my new identity.

As with most children, I loved my mom. Children have the power to see the good in people. Children have the ability to separate a person from his/her actions and love them unconditionally. It is not until we become older that we learn to judge rather than forgive. I learned a lot by watching my mom. Growing up, I could feel her pain when she felt misunderstood and misjudged. It was through her I first witnessed the *second-class-citizen* concept. Second class citizens are those who do not represent the American-dream family. They are those who are typically affected by one of the sins on the *Christian's go-straight-to-hell* list. People without formal education or have obvious mental defects are often included on this list. Like a new car once driven off the lot, your value has immediately depreciated if you are a member. If your parent is a second-class citizen, then you are deemed a second-class citizen.

This social hierarchy is very prevalent in the church. For descriptive purposes, here I will liken the church to Hollywood. Just like Hollywood, many church members from the B-list strive to make A-list status. This can be attained by proving your value and gaining acceptance by A-list members. This is one reason titles are so important in the church. Titles add value. As stated earlier, people have a need to fit in or belong to a group. Everyone wants to be accepted and valued. If you look closely, second-class citizens are some of your hardest working members. If you take an even closer look, you will also notice that second class citizens are also the ones who may drop off the scene, switch churches, or stop going to church altogether. This happens when we begin to believe the lie or accept what others say about us. Sometimes we leave to simply avoid the judgment. We strive so hard to fit in until we forget that God does not use perfect people. We are the unlikely people that God seeks to use to show the world His grace and mercy. Sometimes we work so hard until we lose focus on the true things of God. We strive so hard to be seen as worthy until our true motives shift from living a life that is pleasing to God to working to prove your worth among men, all just to prove that our life does not have to end when we mess up.

Like many in her time, my mom had to leave school when she became pregnant. There was an unwritten concept that if a young girl became pregnant without the prospect of getting married, her dreams were over. Her independence was lost. She was expected to stay at home to raise the child. Very few were encouraged to continue their education. I saw this idea repeated throughout my life. I saw this at home with my mom. I saw this in neighboring families. I saw this in my church. I saw this same concept in my new neighborhood. I understand the need for family support and how this benefits the child, but the real problem is the permanent state of shame and dependence until a prospect came along. Most women either married the next prospect, continued to repeat the same mistake hoping things would be different the next time, or they decide to give up on their personal dreams altogether and make the child and taking care of the home front their central focus.

> Dear Pastor,
>
> What do you do when door number 2 is your lot? Because now, that makes me a second-class citizen.

Whether we like it or not, children receive many messages from the way we interact with them. Children observe many unwritten social rules. Children will learn more from your actions than from your words. As a child, we observe and learn from those in our environment. What we witness and experience shapes our outlook on life. As a child, I learned early that children with fathers had an unfair advantage on life. At that age, I didn't even fully understand why, but still it was very obvious to me that having a father, especially in the household, added value to a child's life. This wasn't anything that I had overheard or had been told. I saw this in my family. I watched as my uncles doted on their little girls. I can remember envying girls who had fathers. You can see the love and adoration. I wanted that.

Therefore, even though we live in the same community and go to the same church, we may have a very different experience than others. Some of us never received the validation (Yes, I said it.) that loved ones bring. We may have received a different message in life. These negative messages and experiences affect our outlook on life and often build doubt and unbelief in our attempt to follow Jesus. Doubt and unbelief are two killers of spiritual growth. Thus, it may be harder for some of us to gain the right perspective—God's perspective. God sees our hearts and knows our purpose. God knows the thoughts He has of peace and not of evil. God knows the expected end he has for us (see Jeremiah 29:11). We need only to trust and believe. How do I begin to achieve God's perspective? I begin by letting go. Let go of whatever binds me to old mindsets. For me, I had to let go of the feeling of unworthiness.

On this journey, one day I had to stop and ask myself what message am I sending the next generation, am I encouraging the next generation to seek the things of God, or am I encouraging the next generation to seek the approval of man? Am I encouraging the next generation to seek their godly purpose or seek the things of the world? If I continue to wear my happy mask, how will the next generation know where God has brought me from? How will they know that they, too, with Philippians 4:13, they can overcome their second class citizenship status? How will they know that only their relationship with God matters? No status is needed. I want the next generation to know that no matter the circumstance, they can place their hope and faith in God. Don't let people count you out.

Lesson 2: Overt Sins Are Rarely and Truly Forgiven

Being raised in the church, I was taught that having children outside of marriage is wrong. (It ranked high on the *Christian's go-straight-to-hell* list along with drunkenness, drug dealing or drug abuse, adultery, gambling, homosexuality, and murder.) Although I was never a promiscuous person or a curious teen, I decided that I no longer wanted to be a virgin. I was simply tired of lying about not being a virgin. So I had sex. The need to fit in won over the little I had been taught about abstaining from premarital sex. It wasn't the hormonal desires of a teenager, but the desire to belong to a group that defeated years of attending Sunday school, singing on the youth choir, family prayers, and regularly attending church.

I do not recall feeling guilty for the act of fornication. I only recall the guilt and shame that set in once I learned that I had become pregnant. I could no longer pretend that I was living the life that I sang about on the choir. I could no longer pretend that *I was the student that was voted most likely to succeed by her senior class* and was on her way to achieve great things. I simply could no longer pretend. I wasn't a bad person. I had just made a bad choice. Even though having an abortion was an option in 1990, it was never an option for me. (After all, abortion is the same as murder, and murder is on the Christian's go-straight-to-hell list. I didn't want to go to hell.) After a couple of months of trying to convince myself that I was only experiencing early menopause at the tender age of seventeen, I had to face reality. I was pregnant. I had sinned.

Like many Christians today, I did not equate premarital sex as the sin. I equated having a child out of wedlock as the sin. This act destroys the image of godly living. This act destroys or at the very least taints the perfect or ideal family. This act immediately places a Christian female on the B-list. Like the scarlet letter, my sin would forever be before me. Still, I acknowledged my sin and accepted my punishment until the s.h.i.t.t. crept in.

During my journey as a pregnant teen in church, I learned a few lessons. I learned that I was no longer a good catch. Mothers want the best for their sons. It didn't matter how hard I worked to raise my son, stay on the dean's list in college, and worked part-time to provide for my family, I was never going to be good enough. It didn't matter that I worked and refused food stamps and welfare. It didn't matter that I chose to keep my baby when others around me chose to end a life. It didn't matter that I didn't smoke, use drugs, or drink. It didn't matter that I didn't indulge in the club scene. None of that mattered.

People of the Christian faith are big supporters of "the right to live." Yet, people of the Christian faith are some of the biggest condemners of children being born out of wedlock. What lesson does one learn when many of her teen friends are on birth control pills? What lesson does one learn when her teen friends have abortions to avoid the ridicule and responsibility of becoming a parent? What lesson does one learn when she observes her friends erroneously retain their image of innocence because of their hidden sin? She learns that Christians fear the judgment of man more than they fear the judgment of God. She learns that Christians have the same mantra as any other people: "We prefer that you do not sin, but if you do, just don't get caught." Because when you do, you are on your own. Becoming pregnant would be another reason for me to have to prove my worth to the world.

At that point, I severed ties with many friends in my life. Not because they were a bad influence on me, but because they unknowingly distracted me from my course of action. After all, it was me against the world. (Yes, I learned many years later that it was really me against myself, but at that point, I was determined that I was going to win in life.) If I really focused and worked hard, I could still have my college degree, career, husband, house, 3.5 kids, and a dog. Therefore, anything or anyone that reminded me of "where I could be if" had to be at least temporarily deleted from my life. I no longer returned letters to my friends who would write me from college, telling me about the college life I was missing. I only kept in touch with two high school friends, one who had decided that the college life was not for her, and another although she had chosen to attend college, I never felt judged or pitied by her. To this day, they are still the ones I call my friends.

My life (or routine) at that point consisted of being a full-time student, working part-time, and being a dedicated mom. I continued to go to church. After all, I believed in raising my family in the church just as I was. I didn't have time to party. (I was such a homebody at one point that even my grandmother told me that I needed to get out of the house sometimes.) I do not think anyone knew that I saw being able to still go to school as a gift from above. Many girls who become pregnant do not get the opportunity to continue their education. I only had to sit out a semester. I was blessed. I did not take it for granted. God had given me a second chance, so I did not mind sacrificing my youthful party years and took on the role of adulthood at the age of eighteen.

All the work and sacrifice paid off when I earned the presidential scholarship the school offered to two students each year, along with other scholarships and awards I received throughout my college career. I was proud to graduate magna cum laude within the normal four years. I did it. I won, another point for my self-esteem and another point that proved that I was just as good as anyone else. (Thank you, God, for blessings after the mess.)

Of course there were some bumps and bruises along the way like when I took by child's father to court for support. After all, it was his responsibility, too. Imagine my amazement when the judge informed me that it was in my son's best interest that his dad finished school. (Not that I had asked him to stop. I asked him to help while he was in school. After all, I had to work and go to college. I did not understand why he could not do the same to help support his son.) Imagine my confusion when I was informed that because he was going to school on a football scholarship and his school was located in a rural area, it would be a hardship for him to work and maintain his schedule. Jobs were limited in his area. Then the judge continued to inform me that I could always apply for welfare as a means of support. Welfare, that was the answer. I was stunned to say the least. There I thought I was going to college for a better life for my family, and the judge suggested I went on welfare.

The system was looking out for my son. The system was looking out for his dad. But who was looking out for me? What message did I receive? I learned that I couldn't depend on anyone. I learned that I was going to have to do it by myself or just become another statistic. I was going to prove to the court, my child's father, and his family that I was more than a statistic.

Well, at the end of the hearing, I was awarded twenty dollars a month in support. (I only received that because I had purchased insurance for my son. The judge felt that was the honorable thing to do.) I was crushed. At that point, I did not know how I was going to make it. The only thing I did know was that I was not going on welfare or food stamps.

Upon exiting the courthouse, I had to hear how my son's father was already giving me money every month, and I was just being greedy. That hurt even worse than the judgment of twenty dollars a month and the suggestion that I apply for welfare. How does one respond to a lie? I didn't respond. I did not see the point in arguing with someone willing to lie to protect a relative's image. At least the act demonstrated that they were embarrassed for not contributing to my son's well-being.

After accepting the fact that I was going to have to do the parenting thing alone, I soon learned that another girl from my neighborhood was expecting his child. Message received: You are easily replaced. During those years, I learned the art of "grin and bear it." Pretend it doesn't hurt when it's actually killing you inside. An act I would have many opportunities to perfect.

After college, he became a real father to my son. I appreciated that. Their close relationship continues today. I can laugh now as I write this, but I recall the years of feeling as if I had the scarlet letter A written on my chest. (Just a friendly reminder to society that I'm not perfect.) I was determined to be a good mother. I remember working extra hard in school and at home to make certain my son had everything he would have if he had been born in the right environment. I made certain that he would behave and perform just as well if not better than children born in the right environment. I laugh at that thought now. What is the *right environment*? Is it the traditional Southern Baptist Church image or definition of family? This view is nothing short of idealism—using one's beliefs or values to represent things as they might or should be rather than as they are—the husband/wife team. The husband is the head of the household, provider and protector. The wife is the wholesome mother, caretaker, and submissive partner. The children are the clay, ready to be molded into the image of their parents and eager to mimic the roles of their parents.

I have witnessed countless members that fit these descriptions. I have also witnessed some of these members leave church once they no longer fit this mold. Why? Because we no longer feel worthy of the church. We have lost our title. We are ashamed of our less than Christian image because now, we are like those whom we deemed less fortunate than us because of their inability to attain the *model* Christian life. We need time to get it right or fix our brokenness— regain our place in life.

Too often, we count our blessings as a result of perfect or right living—not a result of God's favor, grace, and mercy. Our spouses are a result of our accomplishments, beauty, personality, job status, choices, or work. (Unfortunately for many, this is true. This contributes to many divorces. We follow our personal desires and will and adopt the trends of the world.) We mistakenly believe that our children's success is a direct result of our parenting skills—not a result of God's blessing and plans for their lives.

While it is true that God will bless us for staying faithful to His ways, we must remember that God has different paths for His children. Although we may not understand someone else's path, we should not condemn them if their walk appears different. We should remind ourselves that it could have been us born to a crack addict or born into a situation where those who are supposed to protect us misuse us. Would our outlook on life be the same? Would our road to Damascus look the same? We should extend the same compassion that God extends to us each day. We all have tests. We may not be given the same test. We will not all experience the same storm, and my s.h.i.t.t. may be different from yours, but God loves us all the same.

Still, over those early years, I noticed a pattern. Moms truly want the best for their sons. Best means trouble free or less complicated. "You sure you want to date someone with a child?" was what I was often told by a boyfriend—that was the advice given to them. Although it hurt, I understood. After all, I was a mom. I couldn't change the way people thought, but I could prove that I was worthy.

I penned my true thoughts in my journal as I wore my happy-to-fit-in mask to disguise my heart. In 1999, I wrote a poem as a source to vent my experiences without disturbing the natural order of things. After all, it wasn't the world's fault that I had a child out of wedlock. It was mine. I owned that. Still, it hurt. I wanted all those moms to know that I, too, was worthy.

From One Queen to Another

Black queen
The mother of all mothers
Intelligent and strong
Building traditions of her own.
Others try to steal
Your walk
Your talk
Your sassy groove.
Faces of other nations
Mimic your every move.
I walk in your shadow,
And in the rays of your sun.
Your body language speaks how you feel.
Things your tongue would never reveal.
Your demeanor is strong.
How could I go wrong
With tasting a fruit from your tree?

Your son—
The man of my dreams
A strong, black brother
There was never another
Whose power was so great
It could make a queen
Fall from grace.
A young love so beautiful
A queen and her king
Two hearts

Two souls to become one
The American dream.

And baby makes...
Two.

Because now your son is through
He has the right
To seek a more perfect life.
A queen now dethroned
Alone.
A diminishing pride
A new life growing inside
As a part of her grows
A part of her dies.
In church you preach
That abortion is wrong.
Then your turn around
And put me down
And erroneously uplift the voice
Of those who cry,
"It's my choice!"
Their two wrongs
Have made it right.
Now, I struggle
For my dignity I fight.
You tell your sons
I am not the one
For a strong king
Deserves a true queen.

Today I tell you,
If your sons cannot stand up
You need to shut up.
Preaching the gospel of yesterday.
Yet—they are

Hurting from the Inside

Slipping, sliding, sneaking, and creeping
Because of your tongue
Many girls are weeping.
Telling us that we are unworthy
Like a rose with thorns

Beautiful—
But unable to hold
Without being "stuck."
With help from above
True unconditional love.
I made it.
Although you said it
Could not be done.
I won.
A better life
My "thorn" and I
Side by side
And you wonder why
So many die?
In spirit—
Hope and trust?
When all were created in sinful lust.
So why should I worry
About things to come?
About hope for tomorrow?
About things undone?
A life sentence alone
The world has already given me.
Shackled to my choice
Will I ever be free?
Free to love
A king of my own?
Experience worthiness
Or return to my throne?

I stand
Anticipating the realization
That tomorrow may mimic today—
or so it seems.
What happened to my dreams?
The dreams of a black queen.
Do they have to die
When another life if born?
My soul shouts, "No!"
I defy the tongues of those who say so.

Still my journey continues
Like a runaway at night.
Lonely and afraid
But never giving up the fight
For my right to dream
That today I may still be
That beautiful black queen.

Now, like you
For my king I want only the best.
Someone who can withstand
Life's many tests.
An intelligent, strong
Respectable lady—
Just like his mother.
This is my message to you
From one queen to another.

Even though I tried to be a strong example for others, the experience affected my outlook that I eventually carried with me into adulthood.

>Dear Pastor,
>
>What can I do to get off the *Christian's go-straight-to-hell* list?

Lesson 3: Ride the Lie 'til You Die! (Because Image Is Everything)

"...If ye continue in my word, then are ye my disciples indeed; And ye shall know the truth, and the truth shall make you free!" (John 8:31–32).

Sometimes in life, we choose to do the wrong or honorable thing to achieve a right outcome. In other words, we try in our own strength to right a wrong. We find ourselves saying, "I can make it work if I just..." or, "How would it look if...?" This is a snare that most, if not all, fall prey to at some point in their life, image—how things appear to others. If not careful, we will allow image to supersede our truth which leads to bigger problems. I know. I have done this.

During my junior year in college, I reconnected with an ex-boyfriend from high school. He had returned home after serving time in the military and was currently in the reserves. He wanted to rekindle our friendship. Our relationship in high school was the typical innocent relationship. (Typical by the late eighties standards) We had never gone out on a real date in high school. We were both band members, so our dates consisted of sharing a seat on the bus as we traveled to football games.

He was a nice guy from a great family, so why not. ("Why not" was the reason I dated most men at this time in my life.) He treated me with respect, he supported my dreams, he had dreams of his own, and he was family oriented. As with most relationships, the subject of sex eventually arose. I did not object. I only suggested that we wait until I had some form of birth control. I was going to be smarter that time. (See teenagers who equate sex as love become adults who equate sex as love. That was true of me. I still did not see sex as the sin at that point in my life. Although I did not indulge in it, I did not completely abstain from it either.)

Dear Pastor,

I guess by now you have figured out that I spent most of my early adult life seeking that I did not have as a child. How do you help a young girl crying out for love?

Well, once again, history repeated itself. Being from a Christian background himself, my now ex-husband immediately wanted to do the *right thing* and marry me. I suggested that we wait because I was still in college and had no way of contributing to a household. My part-time job would not be enough. I convinced him to wait because money was a major contributor to most divorces, and I wanted to finish college before getting married.

After the birth of our daughter, he proved to be an excellent father. He was very hands-on in her care. He volunteered to keep her routinely certain nights to share the responsibility and to make my last semester in school less stressful. When it came to his daughter, I didn't have to ask for anything. My only challenge was that he would often complain that by not marrying him, I was causing him to be a part-time dad, something he never wanted to be.

Although I did not want to be married, I eventually decided that it would be the best for everyone, especially my daughter. My daughter would have the one thing I had always wanted, a dad—a dad who loved her and treated her like his little princess, like the dads on TV. There was no way I was going to deny my daughter a relationship with her dad. I had always felt that I was wrongfully denied the opportunity to have a relationship with my father. I knew the pain. I would not be guilty of the same crime.

During that time of contemplation, I was reminded by a close family member that I would soon be going on interviews seeking a teaching job. It would look better if I were married with two children instead of single with two children. Honestly, I had already addressed the same issue to myself. I knew that although I had excelled in my studies and craft, loved school and children, and came from a Christian background, that would not negate the obvious character flaw. A young black single mother of two was not the best image for teaching in a Southern predominately white school. Once again, I was afraid that my true worth and hard work would be overshadowed by the fact that I had children out of wedlock. Yes, getting married would make everything better for everyone involved.

Did I love him? Yes. Was I *in love* with him? No. Did I feel that he was the one? No. Could I make this work? Yes. Did I plan to spend the rest of my life with him? Yes. Was this what I dreamed of? Of course not, but it was the right thing to do.

For me, getting married was a compromise, so there were a few things I wasn't comfortable with doing. One, I did not want to get married in a church. Never would I tell that lie in God's house. Although he wanted a small church wedding, I quickly reminded him that we could not afford a church wedding and that getting married at the courthouse would be faster and more cost efficient. Two, I did not pretend I was the excited bride-to-be. I did not immediately tell anyone, not even my mom or my close friends. I hadn't really accepted the idea of becoming someone's wife; therefore, I didn't want to talk about it. I was not excited. I was more like a willing participant, but I never felt forced. I knew I had options. I prayed that no one noticed the ring that I would sometimes wear. It wasn't what I wanted to do. It was what I felt *obligated* to do. Obligation is that feeling we get when we want to do the right thing by someone's design. In not wanting to be the bad guy or send the wrong message to key people in your life or the person you *owe*, we allow external pressure to lead to internal pressure which leads to feeling obligated. Unfortunately, this also leads to dishonesty.

With two words, "I do," the love I had turned into instant resentment. Never had I resented someone so much. All I could focus on were the things that I had discovered that he wasn't totally honest about before we were married. I was honest about my finances; he was not. He expected me to financially help him go to school. We never discussed that before the marriage. I couldn't help but think, "No one helped me. Why should I help you?" Our living arrangement wasn't what he had promised. Everything had changed. He had changed. I felt deceived. All I could see was his dishonesty that led to my unhappiness. I was willing to live with my lie. I wasn't willing to live with his. Mentally, I was done after four months. Physically, I stayed in my marriage for a year and a half before I found the courage to leave. I finally decided that I would rather be a single mother of two than continue to live that lie. Suddenly, I didn't care how it looked. My life and happiness became more important than my image.

For the first time, I felt like I had a voice. I was proud that I stood up for myself. His words from our last argument continued to resonate in my ear: "We're married now; there's nothing you can do about it." That depressing thought stung my soul. "There's nothing you can do about it." I had to find a way out. Otherwise, my life truly didn't matter.

Although it did not take long for me to acknowledge that my marriage was a lie, it took almost fifteen years for me to acknowledge that it was my pattern of behavior that led to me agreeing to marry when I clearly did not want to be married. For years, I blamed my ex-husband for our failed marriage—he had changed. He had not been honest. The real problem, *I* was not honest with myself. I was a people pleaser with low self-esteem. I did not think I could do better. I believed the lie. Therefore, I was willing to settle for what others thought was good enough for me when I wanted more for myself.

I felt victorious when God showed me one of my tragic flaws. I saw how I made life-changing decisions based on the fear of being rejected and trying to please other people. If I didn't think I was worthy of better, why should anyone else? With two kids and a failed marriage, I knew it was going to be hard, but still I knew I could have my "happily ever after." Again, I was determined to win. That time I was armed with a little more courage or so I thought.

The Lie Continues

When I left my marriage, I returned home to live with my grandmother. She was very understanding and supported my decision to divorce. We made a great team. She helped me raise my children, and I helped with the bills and much needed repairs. During that time, I focused on my children and their extracurricular activities, my career, and church. The three Cs kept me pleasantly busy. Although I had to wait a year and a day before I could get a divorce, I was content that part of my life was behind me. Again, I encountered bumps and bruises, but for me, those were just minor setbacks. They were nothing compared to the mental prison I had just received a pardon from. So I kept the little things in perspective. I was free. Nothing else mattered.

As time passed, I was ready to try my wings and move out on my own. Although I was only gone for a short year and a half, I had grown accustomed to the idea of having my own household. I had never really been out on my own. During my abbreviated marriage, we lived with his parents. It was my turn to try my wings. I was ready to begin a new chapter, and then it happened.

Tell me, what does one do when the grandmother who raised you, stood by you when you gave birth to your first child, gave you your first vehicle to drive, let you move back in—no questions asked—when your marriage failed, kept your child at no cost while you went to college, took in your siblings when they did not want to live with their new stepfather asks you to take over her house as your own instead of buying your own place? You say, "No."

At least that was what I did initially. I said, "No." The reason I shared with her was that it would be hard for family to adjust to the idea that I then owned the family house. I was afraid that my wishes would not be respected when it came to property matters. My family and I would not have privacy. Everyone was accustomed to coming and going as they pleased. That would not be the ideal arrangement for my family. Besides, as a teacher, I could not afford two households (because my plans remained the same—to move out). So I offered her the opportunity to move in with me. After all, she was giving me the property in which to put my house. She asked me again to think about it because the house was already willed to me upon her death. She understood my concerns and assured me that she would inform the family of our new arrangements. She would make certain that my family wishes would be respected. She further explained that she felt that this arrangement would be easier for us both, and she honestly did not want to start over at that place in her life.

My grandmother is not one to ask anyone for anything. So to hear her ask for help was humbling. I had to take a look at my actions. Here is a woman who never turned her back on family—children or grandchildren—especially me. She always included me as one of her children—not grandchild. She had always encouraged me to succeed and I did. How could I simply walk away since that I had achieved the things that I could not have done without her support? She had taken care of me for so many years. Why can't I return the favor? Did I feel pressured? No, I felt obligated.

I was so proud to take on the role of provider, especially to someone who had provided for me for so many years. I felt blessed— chosen to have the opportunity to return the love shown to me over the years. Not only had I made my grandmother happy, but I felt that God was proud of me that I was selfless. Then life began to teach me a timeless lesson. I cannot seek the things of God and have the things of the world, too.

"For my thoughts are not your thoughts, neither are your ways, saith the Lord, For as the heavens are higher than the earth, so are my ways higher than your ways, and my thoughts than your thoughts" (Isaiah 55:8–9).

It was not long before I figured out that I had just committed *social suicide*. Many options and my independence died at age twenty-seven. The freedom and equality that I had worked so hard for somehow ended when I signed the papers. Because at that moment, I had unknowingly agreed to forever remain a second-class citizen. What I failed to realize until later was that because I had two children and a failed marriage (if you can call it that) I was chosen to take care of the home front—door number 3. By seeking the wrong acceptance, I unwittingly allowed people to count me out.

Dear Pastor,

My s.h.i.t.t. is beginning to stink. I agreed to live my life looking out from a cave. No, I did not have to, but I agreed to all in the name of doing the right thing.

During this time, I lived and breathed Galatians 6:9, "Be not weary in doing good for in due season you shall reap a reward if ye faint not." I had to believe God will not forget me. I had to believe something. Surely, he would see my hard work and sacrifices and bless me, too, surely. Being the faithful God that he is, he did bless me. I was blessed with both a master degree and national board certification in early childhood education, not bad for a second-class citizen and two more points for my self-esteem.

New problem: No matter how many degrees or awards I achieved, I still lived with my grandmother. No matter how many bills I paid or what my name was on, it was still her house. So now what? I really believed that it could work for the both of us. We worked together well in the past. Why wasn't the arrangement working as well? Oh yeah, I had grown up. I had dreams of my own.

My desire to move out on my own did not die. It was only suppressed by my busyness. Thankfully, the duties of raising two children, work, school, and church kept me too busy most days to focus on what I did not have. Actually during those days, I felt blessed to be single—one less responsibility to manage.

Dating during that era was enlightening. The biggest lesson that I learned was that men liked convenience and accessibility if you will. Even the *good* men wanted the option of staying over even if sex wasn't the immediate goal. That really was not an issue for me because I did not believe in having men around my children. My children were not going to have temporary uncles. If I did not see real potential in a relationship, I usually ended it quickly. Or if I felt that the guy wasn't truly interested, I did not hang around. I did not believe in chasing love. Closed doors are welcomed doors. I believe everyone deserves to be loved—not used.

I came in contact with many successful young men who showed interest. I soon learned that I would save myself a lot of grief if I looked toward dating older men. The reason, men between the ages of twenty-seven to thirty-five are establishing themselves and building their financial identity. Surprisingly to me, my having two children was not a deal breaker. I was financially independent and responsible, and I did not come with baby daddy drama. The deal breaker was that I had my own household to maintain, and I was not willing to forfeit those financial responsibilities. Simply put, I could not afford two households. I could not financially contribute to the dream. That would put a big dent in attaining the image of success, major deal breaker.

Only once do I recall seriously considering forfeiting my promise in order to relieve my finances. I had the opportunity to relocate closer to my friend to better establish our relationship. We both wanted a more normal relationship. I eventually decided against the move, citing that it would be a burden for everyone involved. We continued our long-distance relationship until we decided to just be friends. We remained friends for many years. Later, he would become my back-pocket friend (Break the glass in case of emergency). Was that the relationship that I wanted? No, but with my circumstances, it was the one that I had. Although the single life treated me well, still I secretly had hopes of finding Mr. Right and having a normal family life. Those were desires I kept hidden behind my happy mask.

Game Changer

Up until that point, most of my relationships or acquaintances only lasted for one to three months, no major heartbreaks. I always had a low tolerance for drama or crap. I was never one for emotional rollercoaster rides. When the ride would start to go downhill, I simply got off. I knew what I wanted. I didn't see the point in wasting anyone's time. Physical attraction was never enough for me. I needed a real connection and someone on the same page that could handle my situation. I knew that would not be easy. I was patient.

Sometimes there was an overwhelming feeling that God had something greater for me. I had to be willing not to settle for anything less. No, I was not looking for perfection because I myself had fallen short. Nevertheless, the feeling that there was something greater enabled me to walk on. For some reason, I was unable to buy into the idea that all men were dogs, and people should just give up on true love and live for the moment. The God that I served did not intend for his child to live alone. He had something greater for me. I had faith. I could still win. I approached each relationship with this attitude: I could still win. (My happy mask would not be in vain.)

I still remember how amazed and excited I was when I was approached by my next suitor. He was a single, independent, hardworking male who owned his own home. He already knew of my living situation, so that would not be a hurdle for me to cross. He also knew that I had children—no shockers there. He was nine years my senior and past the establishing-himself stage of his life—another plus for me. He had a good reputation, and he attended and worked in an area church regularly. He was past his player days and was more focused on his jobs which included self-employment. I was accustomed to being approached by good men, but that particular suitor was more than I would have ever expected. I had seen him many times before, but I would have never expected him to be interested in me. He was definitely considered one of the eligible bachelors in the community. He did not have any children, and he was attractive. Was God smiling down on me or what? That was what I have been waiting—excuse me—praying for. That was such a great fit for me. Just the idea of dating him added value to my life.

As with most relationships, the getting-to-know-you stage was wonderful. He proved to be the gentleman that I knew he would be. I did not feel that emotional or spiritual connection that I thrived for, but I did not let that deter my blessing. I was lucky to be with him (Yes, I said lucky because this was my mindset at that time.). The connection could come later. I enjoyed our dates, and how I felt hanging out with him. I truly felt special—like I had been given a pass. Even though at that point in my life I was not looking to get married any time soon (the residue of my last marriage had not completely washed away), I was looking for a healthy, monogamous relationship that could potentially lead to marriage. I did want someone I could potentially build a life with. Then without warning, the game changed.

I was waiting for him to pick me up to attend the local high school football game. When it was past the time he would have arrived, I called to see if everything was okay. That was when he informed me that he was already at the game, and he did not know that we were riding together that week. I was lost. I did not understand why that week was different or confusing to him. I spent the drive to the game wondering what had I done to bring about that sudden change. Maybe I had not shown him enough interest. (I did have a busy schedule.) Maybe I needed to step up my game. After arriving at the game, I sat with my friends after he gave me the not-now-I'm-talking-to-my-friends look. After the game, he explained to me that we did not always have to ride to the games together or sit together to be friends. Ok, I thought, a little different, but if I just hang in there I could see where it was going. After all, he was a good man. You didn't just walk away that easily from a good man.

Over the next few months, I slowly began to watch him take away any act that would make it look like we were in a relationship. Public dates were almost nonexistent. I was allowed to visit him at his house. I had to be understanding because he did have his lawn service to maintain after he completed his day job. I couldn't be one of those selfish girlfriends who complained that their significant other worked too much. He was busy before our friendship, so I had to accept that. We would go to the movies or out to eat on occasion. I had to be patient. He was an older man, so he was probably set in his ways.

Next, our conversation changed. "I thought about it, but I just didn't" would become an all too familiar phrase that I would hear too many times over the next years. This phrase would explain why we did not do the normal things people in a relationship would do. At one point, I was even told to "leave my heart on the shelf or dresser." As harsh as that sounded, I understood. Hurt people are cautious people. Having been hurt before, I understood the process and the need for me to have patience for my friend to heal. I told myself that I had to learn how to deal with the bad as well as the good if I was ever going to have a real relationship that lasted more than three months.

He was not big on hugs and kisses or holding hands. That was okay. I was not used to those things anyway—not used to people being in my personal space. (Actually, I had grown to hate it. If you were over the age of twelve, back off! No hugs allowed!) When I asked if he loved me, his only response was "Would I cut your grass for free if I didn't love you? I don't cut anyone else's grass for free." Even though I wanted more, I had to accept that because after all, love is an action word. He was not out in the streets or clubs. He was not out with other women. I was the one he chose to spend time with. Unfortunately, I would spend the next six years defining our relationship by deductive reasoning and trying to convince myself that everything would work out if he could just or if I could just… I spent the next six years spending holidays alone because we decided to spend time with our own family and just see each other later that night. (At least that was the lie I told because I was not invited.) That would soon become a very familiar lie because he often chose not to accompany or support me as a significant other would. Because I had always been Ms. Independent and Ms. Do It Yourself, it was an easy lie to tell and believe. I never left home without my happy mask.

Moment of Truth: The first time I was around his family was at our baby shower three years into our relationship. I told myself that that was okay because technically, I already knew his family, no big deal. Did I have my baby to trap him? No, I had always wanted three children. I always thought three was the perfect number of children. I knew we were not getting married anytime soon, but I was in my early thirties and I did not want to wait too late. At that point, I was not sure if I would ever marry again, but that was not going to stop all of my dreams. I know many women can relate to the strong desires to have a baby. That was the place I was in—seeking a purpose, love, and happiness. For me, having a baby gave me all three. I needed a new purpose in life. I wanted love and some happiness. I deserved some happiness.

Although my relationship was not anything I wanted it to be, I held on to the dream that one day it could be if he would just… I believed in communication, so even though I did not share my unhappiness with others, I shared them with him. I told him how I felt unloved by him. I even told him that for the first time, I knew what it felt like to be lonely. I was absolutely starving for attention. It seemed like the more I asked for, the less I got. Therefore, I learned not to ask. Then one day, he verbally confirmed what I already knew in my heart—I wasn't what he wanted.

Why do we continue to marry or stay in relationships with people that we know we do not truly love or where we aren't truly loved? We work hard to prove our love and devotion to our chosen one when we clearly hear our spirit tell us to move. Something's not right. Let it go.

Why?

- Lack of faith
- Doubt
- Trusting God only with our words rather than our actions
- Uncertain of the future
- Afraid of change
- Staying with the familiar because it's easier
- "I can make this work."
- "If I just…" or "If he/she just…"
- "I have too much invested in this relationship to give up now."
- Trying to hold on to the image of happiness
- "Should I try harder, or let it go?"
- Or is it because we never truly learned how to first love ourselves?

At the end, I had to ask myself why did I spend eight years in a relationship in which I knew I was not valued or truly loved, why? I believed the lie. I was *lucky* to be with him. He was a good man, so it must have been me. I was willing to compromise my true desires because I feared that I may never find better. I was not even certain if I was worthy of better. I was not good enough for what I truly wanted. I did not feel worthy of such love. That was reserved for prettier people or more perfect people. I was neither. Simply put, I did not value myself.

I always knew that all of the excuses were just that—excuses. After I had already spent six years trying to prove my worth, I spent another two years refusing to admit my defeat. Pride. Pride kept me from letting go when I knew there was an obvious foundational crack in my relationship. I was more concerned with how it would look to those around me than what it was actually doing to me.

I knew my desires were wrong. I began to literally hate myself when I was with him. I hated my need to be with him. It was not even a physical need. It was an emotional need. I felt myself dying inside. I hated myself. The last time I was with him, I felt so ashamed until I cried. I remember sitting in my car in the driveway and just crying. I could no longer justify sex as love. It clearly wasn't. Something did not feel right. I was at war with myself. I needed help. That night, I cried for God to give me the strength not to continue down that wrong path. I asked God to take away my feelings of unworthiness and help me to see myself as He sees me. God did in one night what I couldn't do for myself in two years. He took away my wrong desire to use sex as love. After eight years, I was finally free.

Lesson learned: Real love is not earned. It is a gift from God. We cannot earn God's love. Love is an action word. We do for others because we love. We serve God because we love and trust Him—not to earn His blessings and love. He gives it freely. That is how God loves us. That is how God wants us to love. If you are working to earn someone's love or to prove your love, it just may not be true love. True love is unconditional. It is not based on what someone does for you. If they never do anything for you, you still love them. Love and action come hand in hand. You cannot love someone without doing, but you can do (the action) without love. That is why we should make sure we have God first and allow His spirit to guide us. "Sometimes God's blessings are not in what He gives; but in what He takes away. Trust God" (Anonymous).

Observations from the pew: Church folk are the guiltiest of sticking to a lie for the sake of appearance. If we make a choice (even if it is destroying us inside) we are more likely to stick to it than people in the world. Church folk are more likely to put appearance over personal well-being, thinking God is going to bless us for enduring rather than letting go of our desires and simply trusting Him. We hold on to negative forces in our lives as long as it serves as a positive image on the outside. We spend the rest of our lives making the most of a mess we have made. We never truly give our troubles to Him. We hold on because it's our mess. Deep down, we know that we contributed to our situation; therefore, we feel as if we have to fix it or just deal with it. We never allow God to help us through our mess and move forward to what He has for us.

Dear Pastor,

Since moving away from this phase of my life, it is hard to stay in church and watch younger Christians make the same mistakes that I have made. Like a parent of a rebellious teen, we feel that any words of wisdom will only fall on deaf ears. So we sit back and watch the train wreck of life occur in slow motion before we offer words of experience or encouragement. How wonderful it would be if we could embrace and encourage the next generation in Christ without the fear of judgment from either side! Know that I say these words in love and humility. Just a few notes from the pew.

Exiled

Having experienced repeated disappointments and finally accepting that my life may never be normal, I would spend the next five years immersed in my children, church, and school. (Children, church, and school were things I loved and I was pretty successful at doing.) I began tutoring two to three days after school. At that time, my two oldest children were in high school and would soon be on their way to college. I was busy helping my youngest son adjust to starting school and developing a new routine. Following my oldest son as he played football in high school and in college thankfully kept date night occupied. I looked forward to supporting all of their extracurricular activities.

My church duties also increased during that time. I continued to work with the youth ministry, and I also joined the hospitality ministry. My pastor asked me to teach Sunday school (an opportunity that could not have come at a better time). Although I loved attending Sunday school and I loved teaching, I was not quite sure I was ready for such a great responsibility. After much contemplation and doubt, I decided that if the pastor had that much faith in me, I should at least have a little faith in myself and give it my best try. Teaching would require that I set aside more time to study. I welcomed that. It also provided me with biblical messages to send my oldest son when he was having trouble adjusting to his new college life. Moreover, my work as a Sunday school teacher led me to work with the drama ministry—a job I absolutely fell in love with because it allowed and encouraged me to use my creative gifts in a ministry.

My summers were spent coordinating and volunteering with the church's summer camp for the youth in our church and community. For me, volunteering every summer at camp was personal. It was my way of giving back. Being one of five children, I know summers can feel extremely long when the usual hustle and bustle of school duties is interrupted by long, uneventful days of house chores. And at sixty to seventy-five dollars per week per child, going to a traditional summer camp was not even an option. I wanted every child to experience something different during the summer and to have an experience to write about when they returned to school. Camp also provided an affordable option for parents with multiple children.

I felt so focused during those years. I felt as if my life had a purpose. Truthfully, I felt *empowered*. Being single allowed me to truly dedicate my time and talents with very little external conflict. *I* could really do all things through Christ. By that time, I had perfected being alone. I had no problem with going to the movies by myself (an act that drove my sisters and girlfriend crazy) or just simply staying at home. Once again, I put all my focus on the three Cs: church, children, and career. For so long, I found joy in all three. I did not have time to complain or focus on what I did not have. I had a lot. I lived a blessed life. During those years, I did not look to the left. I did not look to the right. I looked straight ahead, leaving no room for more disappointments.

> Dear Pastor,
>
> This is what the beginning stages of lost hope looks like. We turn away and busy ourselves to avoid dealing with reality. We make substitutions when we fall short of our dreams and true desires. In an effort not to lose, we take control of our lives forgetting that our lives belong to God. He is in control and not we ourselves. We sometimes become super Christians to mask the pain that we are

truly feeling. It may be hard to detect us because we are wearing our happy masks.

Fight or Flight

Sometimes we do not know the effect our actions and words have on people who are trying to cling to hope. Our words and actions have the power to help a person hold on or push them over the edge. As seen in James 3: 8–12, the tongue can definitely be a two-edged sword. With our tongue, we bless God and curse men. Our words have the power to lift up other's spirit. Our words also have the power to kill a person's spirit and hope. Sometimes we feel the need to leave the church to protect ourselves from those stab wounds to our spirit.

The fight or flight theory, as first described by Walter Bradford Cannon, describes the human physiological response to harmful events or attacks. This response tells how we react when we are faced with perceived danger: will we stand and fight or run?

Although this theory is based on the primitive human nature to preserve oneself when faced with eminent danger, the fight or flight theory can also describe how we respond to any situation that threatens our well-being or security, even in the church. Will we stay and stand our ground, or will we leave? Will we keep the faith, or will we give up hope? After forty-two years of church, five and a half years of celibacy, and a life time of s.h.i.t.t., I was ready to run. I was tired of fighting. I no longer saw the purpose. I needed an escape from my bleak existence.

> Dear Pastor,
>
> I give up. It hurts too much to stay. Sometimes I feel like leaving is the only option. I cannot change people. I cannot change my lot in life. I can only change my perspective and accept my lot and move on. I have been fighting to stay within these walls. I have been reading day and night trying to find the words to hide in my heart to be ready for battle for when the thoughts of leaving cross my mind. It vexes my spirit when first-class citizens selfishly hurt me and continue as if everything's okay.

Please tell Christians that saying "forgive me for whatever I have done" is not a true apology or confession of one's sin when they know exactly what they have done to hurt a fellow worshipper or anyone. We use those words when our spirit convicts us of our sins, yet we do not want to truly accept responsibility or the fact that we have sinned and hurt someone. We refuse to say what we have done. Like Adam and Eve in the Garden of Eden (see Genesis 3:7) and David sending Uriah to the forefront of battle (see 2 Samuel 11:6–13), we try to cover our sin. We refuse to call it what it is. We prefer and sometimes even ask that the people we have wronged just get over it. Their first concern is keeping their perfect Christian image before others. They are not willing to walk in their truth.

They hide to avoid the condemnation that they so quickly give to others. Please, pastor, help us see that often times, covering our sin is worse than the sin itself. Covering our sins prevents us from truly being forgiven.

I finally understand why people who have faithfully attended church all of their life suddenly leave the church—not a church, but *the church*. They have lost their hope. These hypocritical actions disturb the spirit. It makes the fight to stay even harder. We are not always as strong as we would like to be. Like Simon Peter in Luke 5:5, we are tired from working and seeing nothing happen, working to no avail. Yet we work and like Jeremiah, we watch others prosper. I am tired of doing good just to be wronged. I am tired of pretending I don't hurt when I am wronged by other church members. I know God's plan is perfect and eventually, everything will work for the good. I know God's word is true because I have seen Him come through for others, so why has he forsaken me?

I am in a state of confusion. Although I live and breathe church, sometimes I feel as if I don't belong. I do not fit in. I am no longer a slave to the flesh or to the world, so I do not always fit in with those who accept Christ but still sow to the flesh. Yet, I do not want to become part of the problem—the traditional, judgmental Christian. So what's the point of trying to live a life that's pleasing to God if I'm only going to be condemned for doing so? For example, I make a point of avoiding tempting situations whenever possible just to be told that I think I'm too good to hang around them or I think I'm better than they are. I do not think I am better. I just don't have a desire to drink. I don't have a desire to go clubbing. I don't have a desire to have sex with men that I know don't love me or men that aren't committed to me. When I was younger, I used sex to feel loved. I know better now, so I put away that misconception. God, himself, took that away from me. I thank Him today for saving me and healing me in that area. So why must I be criticized for not participating in fornication when the Bible clearly states that it is wrong. I am constantly hearing how I am trying to fulfill the law through my works. I am simply trying to be obedient to His word and keep His commandments. Keeping God's commandments is taboo today. I believe in Jesus Christ. I know that He died for our sins, but I do not believe that gives me a pass to live any way I want because of His grace and mercy. I was taught that we should live righteous and stay in God's will. Well, today I hear that the church is not for the righteous, it's for those who believe who are in sin. Doesn't the Bible say both? I believe wholeheartedly that the church is for sinners (which we all are) to hear God's word, to learn of His ways, and to believe that He is the one true living God who is able to do anything. Once we confess and repent of our sins and confess that Jesus Christ is Lord, He will forgive us as though we have never sinned before. We are new in Christ. We have the Holy Spirit to guide us if we let Him.

In today's church, we have people who confess Christ as their savior, who focus on the image of Christ-like living but boldly continue the ways of the world. They preach that they are covered by God's grace and mercy. I know we are no longer under the law, but Jesus did not come to condemn the law but to fulfill the law and through Him we all can be saved (see John 3:17; Matthew 5:17). No man can keep the law. I know that. But if God has saved me and given me the Holy Spirit to lead me in all of His ways, then why should I be condemned by those in the church who still choose to follow their natural self rather than the spirit? I am constantly reminded that it is not of my works. It is through God's grace and mercy. I truly understand this, but because I love the Lord, I choose to follow His will and His ways. I love God because He cared enough for me to take me out of harm's way. He gave me His spirit to comfort and guide me, so I choose to follow His ways. He gives me a choice. No, I am not perfect, but I do try to live righteous. Am I not supposed to? Or am I supposed to follow my own will because I know I am sealed by God's promise to never leave me nor forsake me? I have assurance of heaven because I can never lose my salvation. It is not of my works; it is solely God's grace and mercy. He has already paid for every sin I will ever commit. There is no condemnation for me. Hmmm, so why am I trying to live God's will when I can lie, fornicate, commit adultery, steal, get drunk, be a hypocrite, murder, envy, practice idolatry, cause wrath, etc., as long as I pay my tithes and attend church regularly. I am still going to heaven because Jesus paid it all! So much for walking in the spirit!

I hated thinking that way. I knew my thinking was wrong, but I was in a negative place. I was consumed with anger. I did not want to be, but I clearly was. When one looks deeper into the fight or flight theory, one will see that fight or flight heightens fear and focuses on short-term survival. For me, that meant avoiding the confrontations that were just going to lead to me being misunderstood and leaving the church to regain my focus. We quit during that time because we think God has forgotten us. So many of us leave during that period, convinced that we are right because we see so much that is wrong within the church. We see Christians behaving badly then covering their sins to maintain their image. We see Christians who unfortunately are quick to judge and condemn others. We see people who are hurt by those who call themselves children of God only to be told to "get over it." We leave to heal only to carry our unresolved pain with us. We use our pain to build a wall around us, a fortress built of hurt and pain that blocks anyone else from getting too close. It blocks words that can further tear down our spirit of hope and trust. Eventually we see that our fortress also blocks us from the very thing we seek—God's face. But because Jesus promised in Matthew 17:20, "Because of your unbelief: for verily I say unto you, if ye have faith as a grain of mustard seed, ye shall say unto this mountain, Remove hence to yonder place: and it shall remove; and nothing shall be impossible unto you," even when I wanted to leave, I couldn't.

It was during that time I had to use my mustard seed faith to stay in this race and fight. I wanted to quit so badly, but something would not let me stay away. Although I was in a place of confusion, I knew my thoughts were wrong. I had lost focus. I was too focused on what other people had and what other people were doing. I was too focused on the things that I had lost rather than the things I had gained. I identified with David in Psalm 37. Like Jeremiah, I had asked God how long was He going to let the wicked prosper. Like Jeremiah, I felt that my work was in vain. I had lost my purpose for the ministry. Like Simon Peter, I felt I had toiled all night in vain. I no longer felt like continuing in my ministry. I was tired of working to no avail. I tried hard not to have the self-righteous spirit of Job. I could clearly see my wrong outlook, but I could not change it. I was consumed for three months with anger. I did not want to be angry. I knew the dangers of being angry. Lord, how do I let go of the anger?

I could not escape it no matter what I did. I went to church angry. I stayed home angry. I would leave town angry. I prayed that God would take this anger from me. I couldn't do it alone. I prayed for God to tell me what He wanted me to do. I told Him that He would have to make it plain because I didn't have anything left to give. "I need to know, God, that you love me, too."

The next morning, I prayed again that the Lord would send me a word to guide me through the day with a positive spirit. I turned on the TV as I so often did to watch *Joyce Meyer Ministries* before I left for work. That morning, she spoke about shallow Christians—wanting fruit, not caring about the roots, Christians who want to be used, but don't want to be prepared. She spoke from Luke 5. In that chapter, when Jesus arrived the fishermen (disciples) had already been fishing all night and had caught nothing. They were tired. Jesus tells Simon Peter to "launch out into the deep, and let down your nets for a draught." Simon Peter was already tired from fishing all night to no avail when Jesus tells them to go back but this time step out into the deep waters. Although they were tired, they were obedient to Jesus's command, and they caught a multitude of fishes. The Bible states that they caught so much fish that their nets broke. Not only did they fill their ship, but their partner's ship, too. Both ships were so full that they began to sink (see Luke 5:1–7). Wow, what a God!

Message received: Don't be a shallow Christian. Be willing to step out into the deep. Work even when you get tired. You may not feel like it, you may not see it, but follow God's word anyway. Don't live by what you want or feel. Live by what He tells you to do even when you don't understand, or it doesn't feel good. These tough times prepare us for greater. The race isn't given to the swift, or the strong, but to the one who endures 'til the end (see Ecclesiastes 9:11).

> Dear Pastor,
>
> The church is supposed to be a safe house. At times, it becomes a source of pain and a threat to our emotional well-being. Help us to stay. Help us see it as a source of hope again. Help us stand and fight the fight of faith.
>
> There are members sitting in your church today who are hurting. They have lost hope. To avoid the pain of disappointment, some no longer desire to hope. They have secretly given up on themselves as they sit filling the pews

with deceiving smiles. They are running on empty. They are simply there out of tradition or desperately waiting on a blessing or for *their change to come.* They are praying that their wilderness journey will soon end or at least is not in vain. As time passes, more hurt and disappointment lead to anger and confusion. This is where the journey in church usually ends.

Today I am thankful that something kept me in church even when I did not feel like going—when everything in me wanted to give up or just quit. I am thankful that God did not give up on me when I did not get it time and time again. Although the process was painful, I can clearly see now that it was necessary in order for me to achieve a better perspective. No, I have not arrived. I have just learned how to view and go through with God.

The wilderness experience, we all try to avoid it like the flu season only to become sickened by the task of working hard to avoid it. We work so hard to try to avoid pain when pain is where we learn to lean, trust, and draw closer to God. We all have a wilderness journey, and like the children of Israel, because of disobedience or lack of faith, some of us will not make it out. We retreat back to our old selves. Encourage us. Help us stay focused. Meet us where we are at. We desperately need the church to be an emotionally safe place once again.

The Healing Process

Facing our truth can be a painful process. That is why we often choose to stay in denial. Even after we come to a realization, it is often still a process before we begin to walk in the truth. We hate to admit that we have made choices that have led to our demise and years of unhappiness. We often play the blame game or the unfortunate victim before we admit that we have helped build our cave and sentenced ourselves to a lifetime of turmoil.

For me, I had to finally be honest with myself and admit that I hated not having a father. I had to stop pretending that big sister was tough and didn't need a dad. I had to admit that it hurt that he never took the time to get to know me. This is where my mask began. I often told myself that I was better off because he wasn't in my life. His absence made me tough and independent. For a long time, I was proud of that.

I finally had to admit that my tough, independent exterior only masked the feelings of unworthiness I carried into my adulthood. I continued to knowingly make poor choices because my feelings of unworthiness caused me to repeatedly compromise and not follow my spirit. I feared losing people if I were honest. If I were honest with what I felt or wanted, I was afraid they would not find me worthy and leave. The ironic part is when I look back, I realize that compromising my integrity has never worked in my favor. I always lost when I went against my spirit. Moreover, not following my spirit only left me angry with myself because then I had no one to blame *but myself.* I couldn't plead ignorance. Compromising only leads to loss. I almost lost myself. This led to much internal conflict.

Finally, I had to admit and confront the fact that the people I thought were looking out for me were really looking out for themselves. I had to admit that my need to please people and my reluctance to confront situations made it easy for them to count me out. I didn't have to stay in my situation. I chose to stay in my situation. I was too afraid to leave. I was too afraid to speak up. Once again, I feared the judgment of man over the will of God. I feared being rejected. At the end of the day, that was my fault. It took many years (sixteen to be exact), but I can finally own that.

Sixteen years. Sixteen years in the wilderness. Sixteen years trying to make other people happy. Sixteen years—angry, lost, and confused. Refusing—no, too scared to confront issues in my life. Afraid I would disappoint people in my life. Afraid no one would understand. Afraid of how things would look. Smiling while I was slowly dying on the inside, I desperately wanted someone to hear my silent screams.

Twenty-seven. That was how old I was when my wilderness journey began. Sixteen years walking in circles taking one detour after the next just trying to avoid my truth, trying to substitute love with work, success, or my tough-girl image. This isn't where I want to be. I knew God had more for me. The last two years were almost unbearable. I was a ticking time bomb. I would literally wake up crazy some mornings ready for war, not a spiritual war but a fight to keep my sanity.

I was tired of "do unto others as you would have them do unto you" just to have the opposite come my way. I was tired of "one day…" I needed a breakthrough *today*.

Over the years, I have suffered many self-inflicted spiritual injuries because of unresolved hurt, and my refusal to confront that which God kept bringing me back to confront. There's no prison like the imprisonment of the mind. I was more concerned with how things would look to man instead of freeing myself so I could receive and achieve the things of God. Although I understood and believed, it took a lot for me to *act* on the principle that I could not please man and God, too. I had to realize that I would never achieve the things of God if I was too busy trying to seek the approval of man.

My experiences and how I dealt with them caused me to become angry with my situations. I was angry because my experiences taught me that I should have been more selfish in life. Ironic, right? Then I learned that I did not have to be more selfish, just more honest with myself.

"For this thing I besought the Lord thrice, that it might depart from me. And he said unto me, My grace is sufficient for thee: for my strength is made perfect in weakness" (2 Corinthians 12:8–9).

During my healing process, I knew God was not happy that I continued to keep silent when He had given me so many words to speak. I kept returning to the same place for a reason, no, not personal desires for I had asked God to just take it away. (Yes, I wanted the easy way out.) Yet, for a third time, I had arrived at that same crossroad in my life, still too afraid to speak the truth—my truth. This time I no longer fear being rejected. I belong to God. (It doesn't get any better than that.) You can reject me. That's okay. I will admit to having some fear of being *misunderstood*. I have learned so much on my journey that I want to share. At times, I feel that I need to share. I know not everyone will accept what God has given me, but I also know that my life's journey can help someone who may be struggling with a stronghold in his/her life. Just like you could see me, I can see you. I can see your pain. I can see through your all familiar mask. I used to wear that same mask. I want to reach out to you, but I don't know how. You may just perceive me as a bitter sister, but I cannot allow my fear of being misunderstood keep me from being obedient to God's will. Fear will limit what God wants to do through me. I am learning not to put limits on what God can do. Every day is not easy. Healing is a process.

I only began to heal when I became tired, tired of wearing my happy mask, tired of pretending everything was okay, and tired of not truly enjoying life because I allowed my s.h.i.t.t. to control my thoughts and actions.

Today I want to walk in the freedom that honesty brings. I strive to walk in my truth—imperfections and all. I want my life to encourage others so they may know that they are not alone in their spiritual battle. I felt so alone at times in mine. The Bible says in Romans 3:23, "For all have sinned, and come short of the glory of God." I thank God for the earthly angels He sent to encourage me on my toughest days. I thank God for the messages He sent my way. I want to encourage others to find their source of discontentment then give it to Jesus. Like me, too many of us are working backward. We are addressing the issues or things that have happened to us. This method only allows for a temporary fix. It's like taking an aspirin for a headache. It will soon return because we have not changed the behavior or thing that is causing the headache. Only when you take time to find what is causing the headaches (usually the *whys* in life) and address that issue will the headaches go away. Aspirins are no longer needed. Like the Bible says, we must examine ourselves and seek to correct our wrongs (see 1 Corinthians 11:28). Lamentations 3:40 states that we should examine our ways and return to the Lord. After all, we can't continue the same behavior and expect a different outcome. This time, I'm ready to win with Christ.

A New Outlook

Life can seem hard when we have to face occasional storms. But as I grew in faith, I saw and realized that those storms were purposefully placed in my life to make me stronger and to draw me closer to God. Along with my blessings, I've learned how to thank God for my storms. Now, I am learning how to thank God for my s.h.i.t.t., for it was my s.h.i.t.t. that caused me to be a witness for God. My s.h.i.t.t. propelled me to walk in my truth. It is my s.h.i.t.t. that causes me to praise Him openly and not in my usual conservative way. It is my s.h.i.t.t. that causes me to stop and share my testimony and life experiences with others. It is my s.h.i.t.t. that makes me seek God day and night. My s.h.i.t.t. moved me from victim to victor. Essentially, my s.h.i.t.t. gave me a new life in Christ.

I choose not to be bitter about the years that I have lost. Instead, I choose to focus on what I have gained. Because of Deuteronomy 30:3–13, I know that God can restore all that I have lost. Isaiah 61:7 tells me that God can give me double for my hurt and pain. I believe Isaiah 61:3 when he said God can give me beauty for ashes. (See, staying in church and staying connected to His Word taught me that.)

Being tough and self-sufficient, it took me a while to get here, but I finally understand what it means to be a new creature in Christ. I now understand that these tests are opportunities to see God. I can see God's grace and mercy in my life even when life is not going the way I had planned. I can see God's plan taking over my life when I finally surrendered my will to Him. Pruning season was hard. (Pruning season is when God removes people and things from your life that will hinder you from reaching your destiny and purpose. The familiar things we hold on to just because they are familiar.) I'm not perfect. There are days when I relapse back to my old desires. But God is faithful to remind me that I belong to Him.

I know I do not have the typical life and that's okay. I do not know what lies ahead, but I am trusting God that it will be great. His plans for me are greater than I can ever imagine, so I have decided to let Him lead and just enjoy the ride.

Lesson Learned: If God does not allow our past to determine our present, then we have to decide that we will no longer allow our past to control our present, our thoughts, and actions. We have to see ourselves as God sees us. He does not see us as second class citizens. He sees us as His children. We are the Ishmaels, Gideons, Gomers, Pauls, and Rahabs of today's society. Although imperfect, we are ready to be used by God for a mighty work. We are His chosen generation. We are His heir. We, too, are worthy.

About the Author

Karen V. Greene is a native of South Carolina. She has worked as an educator for more than twenty years. She currently resides in North Myrtle Beach, South Carolina with her youngest son.

www.ingramcontent.com/pod-product-compliance
Lightning Source LLC
Chambersburg PA
CBHW021452070526
44577CB00002B/369